# Ultimate Beast, Ultimate Battle

## The Tiger's Epic Struggle for Survival

Farhan Khalid

"

The tiger depends on the forest;
the forest depends on the tiger.

"

-*Cambodian Proverb*

# DEDICATION

This work is dedicated to wildlife conservationists
and those involved in making the world
a better place for all living creatures.

*Imagine*

Imagine an animal that is dominant on land, yet entirely comfortable in the water. An animal whose night vision is six times better than a human's. An animal whose paralyzing roar can be heard from miles away. An animal whose low growl or mere scent can cause other creatures to run away in fear. An animal that can wrestle and subdue prey quadruple its own size. An animal itself weighing hundreds of pounds, yet able to stalk its prey silently, brilliantly camouflaged by what is essentially an invisibility cloak in the forest.

This spectacular beast isn't just a figment of one's imagination. Fierce and vicious, yet noble and majestic, the wild tiger has been feared and revered for centuries. But the question is, how many more centuries can it survive?

## Earning its Stripes

Compared to other big cats, the tiger has a very distinct look with its rich orange coat and vivid black stripes. An Asian folk story attempts to explain how the tiger got its stripes. A long time ago, the tiger was the proudest creature in the jungle. The only other animal that could hold a candle to the tiger's strength and power was the water buffalo.

One day, the tiger saw the water buffalo being put to work by a farmer. This perplexed the tiger, so after the work was complete, it just had to ask the water buffalo what was going on. Why would it allow itself to be enslaved by a weak, little man? The buffalo explained that the man doesn't need claws or fangs because the man has something even more worthy: wisdom.

The tiger decided that it had to obtain some of this wisdom, whatever it was. So the next day, the tiger waited until the farmer was out again, and jumped out of the bushes right in front of him. Startled and shaken, the farmer asked the tiger what it wanted. The tiger explained that it wanted some of the man's wisdom, to which the man responded by saying that wisdom is not something he can simply hand over. The tiger was not satisfied with this response, so it insisted.

The man, not wanting to be devoured by the tiger, quickly thought of a plan. He explained that he would give the tiger his wisdom, but incidentally had left his wisdom at home and had to go retrieve it. But before leaving, the man expressed concern that the tiger would eat all the farmer's animals. The tiger stated that it wasn't hungry, but the farmer still feared for his animals' safety...or at least that's what he wanted the tiger to think.

The farmer agreed to go home and get his wisdom only if the tiger would allow him to leash it to a nearby tree. The tiger agreed, and off the farmer went. The tiger waited for hours and hours, but the farmer had fooled it. While there are variations of this story, in one version, the tiger eventually decides to break free. It pushes and pushes against the ropes until they finally break, but not before giving it rope-burn in the process. And this is how the tiger got its stripes.

Of course, this isn't actually how the tiger got its stripes, but this story does shed some light on man's complicated relationship with the tiger. Humans have long feared, and revered, the tiger. Will this beast eat my livestock and attack my family? Is it a creature to be loathed? Is the tiger good for anything other than being a zoo attraction?

In this brief book, I'd like to share some interesting facts about tigers, the current situation involving its dwindling numbers, and what can be done (and is being done) to prevent tigers from going extinct. I'd like to finish by mentioning why all this even matters.

### The Beast

What we often refer to as big cats includes animals belonging to the *Felidae* family, such as lions, leopards, jaguars, cheetahs, and cougars (a.k.a. pumas, mountain lions). Tigers, depending on the subspecies, are the biggest of the big cats. Tigers belong to the *Panthera* genus, and are one of the few big cats with the ability to roar.

A tiger's skeletal structure is light, and its spine is flexible. Tigers are very agile despite having considerable body mass. With broad paws and big shoulders, tigers have the body of a wrestler, yet the stealth of a ninja. It's one thing for a housecat to jump from floor to tabletop without a sound, but imagine a several-hundred-pound tiger silently prowling the jungle.

Tigers can kill animals four to five times their own body weight. One advantage they hold over larger animals like wild cattle is that they possess flexible paws with retractable claws. They're also armed with powerful jaw muscles combined with canine teeth (two on top and two on bottom) that can measure between two and three inches each. The canines make it easy for them to subdue prey, while the sharp teeth in between the canines (known as incisors) are able to cut through and tear even tough meat.

Tigers become very familiar with their territories and use this knowledge to their advantage. They know where they can hide, how they can move silently without tipping off their prey, and where prey tend to congregate. Tigers also have flexibility to squeeze into tight spaces or crouch down very low.

Tigers' sense of sight, sound, and touch are exceptional, which they use in combination to stalk their prey. Their sense of smell is not that good, but they mostly use smell to communicate with other tigers by marking trees and other objects. Tigers are unable to climb trees like leopards can, due to their large size, but they happen to be very good swimmers. All in all, the tiger is a remarkable creature.

## Habitat and Subspecies

Tigers are flexible in terms of habitat. Tigers in the wild typically reside in Asian countries with warmer climates, although one subspecies resides in a frigid region of Russia. They can live in hot, dry climates; tropical, sticky climates; or the cold, snowy forests of eastern Russia. They settle in forested areas.

Tigers can survive in a variety of temperatures, from negative 30 degrees Fahrenheit to over 100 degrees. However, they do require shade in the summer to prevent overheating. Their fur allows them to maintain a steady body temperature of about 99 degrees.

Tigers can live from 10 to 15 years in the wild, and up to 20 years (or slightly longer) in captivity. Sizes and weights can vary drastically between subspecies, so let's take a closer look. Subspecies for known living tigers include the following: Amur, Bengal, Indo-Chinese, Malayan, South China, and Sumatran. Subspecies believed to be extinct are the Balinese, Caspian, and Javan tiger.

The Amur, or Siberian, tiger is the largest of all subspecies. It resides in the far eastern part of Russia. The climate there is colder, so Amur tigers tend to have thicker coats. Fully-grown females can range from 200 to 350 pounds, while males can weigh between 400 and a staggering 660 pounds. Females can measure (from the tip of the nose to the tip of the tail) from 87 to 114 inches long, while males can measure from 99 to 134 inches long. To give you a sense of this length, consider the fact that basketball players in the NBA have an average height of roughly 79 inches (that's 6'7" tall), so even an average-height NBA player laying down would be shorter in length than the smallest Amur tiger.

The Bengal tiger is the greatest in number, and lives in India and a few neighboring countries such as Bangladesh. These countries provide a warmer, more humid climate than what the Amur tiger experiences. Females range from 220 to 350 pounds in weight, while males weigh between 400 and 550 pounds. Females have a total length of 94 to 104 inches, while males have a length of 110 to 120 inches.

The Indo-Chinese tiger is found in Southeast Asian countries like Thailand, Vietnam, and Myanmar (Burma). The bulk are in Thailand. Females can weigh from 220 to 290 pounds, while males weigh from 330 to 430 pounds. In terms of total length, females average 96 inches and males average 108 inches.

The Malayan tiger is found in Malaysia (although it previously existed in Singapore and Thailand as well), and was once considered the same as the Indo-Chinese tiger. DNA testing found that these are actually two separate subspecies. Females weigh between 53 and 194 pounds, while males weigh between 104 and 285 pounds. Females have a total length of 71 to 102 inches, while males range from 75 to 110 inches. As you can see, the Malayan tiger is notably smaller than the Indo-Chinese tiger and other subspecies.

The South China tiger may no longer exist in the wild, but there are a number of this subspecies in captivity. Females weigh from 220 to 240 pounds, while males weigh from 290 to

400 pounds. Females have a total length ranging from 87 to 94 inches, and males from 91 to 102 inches.

The Sumatran tiger only exists on the Indonesian island of Sumatra. Because the Balinese and Javan tigers are extinct, the Sumatran tiger is technically the last remaining Indonesian tiger. Females of this subspecies weigh between 165 and 243 pounds, while males weigh between 220 and 310 pounds. Females range in total length from 85 to 91 inches, while males range from 87 to 100 inches. Compared to most other subspecies, the Sumatran is relatively small (although the Balinese tiger is said to have been even smaller).

Keep in mind that the weights and lengths of tigers can vary considerably depending on what source you refer to, but the above gives you some idea of each subspecies' average size for fully-developed tigers.

### The White Tiger Myth

Contrary to popular belief, the white tiger is not a separate or endangered species. White tigers are technically not albino since albino refers to lack of pigmentation. The whiteness of this particular tiger is caused by a genetic mutation, and it's very rare for this mutation to occur in the wild.

It's rather unfortunate that people have bred white tigers to use as money-making attractions. Naturally, a white-coated and blue-eyed tiger draws a crowd. Keep in mind, though, that breeding white tigers usually means inbreeding -- that is, mating one white tiger with a closely related white tiger -- which raises some ethical questions.

Many conservationists feel that there shouldn't be a concerted effort to conserve white tigers, especially considering that the inbreeding process leads to a high mortality rate. In fact, many products of this inbreeding have birth defects, and many cubs end up dying.

*Hunting*

Tigers' prey includes chital and sambar (types of deer), gaur (bison), and wild boars. Since some of these animals have horns that could cause severe injury, tigers typically attack from the side or back. Tigers have also been known to go after porcupines, sloth bears, baby rhinos, and snakes. Although tigers may venture out and try different foods, they by and large stick to hoofed animals.

Tigers don't typically chase prey. Rather, they silently stalk prey by walking on the tips of their paws, then launch an explosive attack. While tigers have magnificent bursts of speed and strength, hunting success seems to be more based on their ability to tiptoe in utter silence, sneakily making their way closer and closer to the unsuspecting victim before the lightning-quick attack is finally made.

Tigers can do short sprints when giving chase, whereas relatively lightweight cheetahs can put up a longer run at higher speeds. Because of the body weight a tiger must carry, it's unable to put up a long chase. What the tiger lacks in speed and endurance, it makes up for in stealthiness and explosive power. However, a tiger's maximum speed of 30 to 40 miles per hour is nothing to sneeze at. For reference, bear in mind that Olympian Usain Bolt was clocked at about 27.8 miles per hour during a sprint, and he's as fast as lightning.

Tigers kill larger prey with a bite to the throat to crush the windpipe. A large kill can feed a tiger for several days. It will feast on a kill over time, eating up to 60 pounds of meat per day. After a successful hunt, tigers normally drag their prey to a hiding spot to feast on, away from scavengers and other predators. Dragging a carcass is easy work for a tiger courtesy of its powerful jaws, along with massive neck and shoulder muscles.

The success rate for hunts based on observation is reportedly only about 10 percent. It's difficult to ascertain how accurate this is since tigers are elusive and nighttime hunts may have different rates of success. However, it has been observed that a tiger will give up its hunt after being spotted by prey, as a drawn-out chase could prove to be overly exhausting for an animal as large as this.

Tigers make very precise, calculated decisions, rarely making mistakes. Mature, experienced tigers are intelligent enough to know when it's worth it to continue with a hunt and when it's better to let it go. Rather than make a hasty move and risk injury, a tiger would rather pull back to preserve itself for future hunts. Such is the conundrum in which predators find themselves; if they can't hunt, they risk starving to death.

Unlike lions who hunt in packs, tigers normally hunt and eat alone, but there have been observations of several tigers sharing a meal. This is expected with a female tiger and her cubs, but on rare occasions multiple adult tigers have been seen feasting on a single kill, taking turns eating from the prey one at a time. Even though tigers are traditionally seen as strictly solitary, this is not always the case.

### Humans on the Menu?

Do tigers eat humans? It's not in a tiger's nature to consume humans, but there have been cases of man-eating tigers. This can occur either because a tiger has been pushed out of its territory and finds humans and farm cattle to be easy prey, because a tiger was disturbed in its habitat by agricultural workers or fishermen, or because a tiger is injured and cannot go after larger prey. For example, an older tiger with broken canine teeth would have to settle for smaller, easier prey.

Interestingly, but sadly, many attack victims had been crouched over when attacked, so they may have appeared as sitting ducks, so to speak. It should be made clear, though, that only a tiny percentage of tigers can be considered as man-eaters. It's abnormal behavior.

## Mating and Childbirth

When it comes to mating between tigers, it's commonly the female who initiates the relationship. One might suppose this is typical, that females do all the work, but in the case of mating there's the issue of reproduction. Since only the female can give birth, she must at least start the process. Additionally, it could be exhausting for a male to go after a female, especially if she plays hard-to-get, which amusingly has been observed among animals. An energy-drained tiger will have difficulty hunting, so it pays to be patient until a female indicates receptiveness.

One method used by female tigers to communicate receptiveness to mating is by marking nearby plants with their scent. They do so by rubbing their faces against trees or shrubbery. Other methods include increased pacing and vocal cues, such as roaring to attract the attention of males. If more than one male seeks to be her knight in shining armor, the female may be choosy in selecting a mate, as she wants someone who is basically a stable partner and will likely remain in the area.

It can take several attempts over a period of days for tigers to finally conceive, so a male simply passing through town is not an ideal mate. Having a dominant male as her mate also means good genes potentially being passed down to her offspring, not to mention protection for her and the cubs.

Once a mate is found, the male and female will find a secluded area to rest and spend time together. They don't jump into the actual mating right away, and a mature male knows better than to rush it, as a female tiger can become aggressive towards her mate. This same type of behavior has reportedly occurred between humans, as well. The female will indicate readiness by her body position, such as by walking towards the male and getting into a crouching position.

After a tiger becomes pregnant, she can give birth to her litter of cubs in just under four months. A litter typically consists of three to four cubs. During pregnancy, she will try to find a safe place where she can give birth and nurse her cubs. She keeps her cubs hidden during the first couple months for their protection, and they feed off of their mother's milk. It could be two to three months before a tiger cub gets its first taste of meat.

Because of the short gestation period, tiger cubs are born blind and highly-dependent on the mother for both protection and food. In fact, tiger cubs only weigh a few pounds at birth, less than the weight of an average human baby. Despite the fragility of her cubs, the mother tiger has incredible control over her jaw strength when picking up and carrying them by the backs of their necks.

The mortality rate for tiger cubs is relatively high, perhaps due to the shorter gestation period compared to most plant-eating animals, so it's not unusual for a tiger to give birth to multiple litters over her lifetime. Because of the extreme measures the mother takes in hiding and protecting her cubs early on, it's difficult to calculate an exact mortality rate.

When cubs are younger, the mother will hide them while she hunts, but as they get older they will accompany the mother on hunts and learn by example. Cubs also roughhouse with one another to learn combat skills and perhaps let out some pent-up energy. Cubs can be rather playful with each other and with their mother, affectionately nuzzling against her.

Permanent canines don't develop until about 16 months of age. After cubs are old enough to hunt, ordinarily at 18 to 20 months of age, they will often hunt together for some months before finally parting ways to establish independent territories. One reason for this separation may be simply due to supply & demand; there is only so much prey in one area, and an adult tiger needs a considerable amount of meat in order to flourish.

*Home Sweet Home*

A home range is the general area where tigers reside and this area may be shared. A territory is a portion of the range that is held exclusively by a tiger (or a few tigers). A territory is the tiger's home, which it will defend against intruders and where it will hunt for food. Related female tigers tend to settle near one another, essentially as next-door neighbors, whereas males tend to scatter far and wide.

Tigers will mark their territories by rubbing their faces against trees and bushes, as well as by secreting a fluid that appears to be urine, but is actually more chemically complex. When other tigers smell this fluid on trees and such, they can get an idea of what type of tiger left the marking. It creates sort of a profile for that tiger.

Tigers aren't as vocal as lions. They may roar out of anger or frustration, as a mating call, or as a call to retrieve their cubs. One study found that tigers can also emit low-frequency sounds known as infrasound (i.e. less than 20 hertz). Humans would not be able to hear such low-frequency sounds, but could supposedly feel it. Thus, infrasound might be another way for tigers to communicate with one another, whether it's to indicate location or audibly mark their territory. Some have suggested that infrasound incorporated in a tiger's roar can literally have a paralyzing effect on prey. Infrasound can travel far, even in a dense forest.

As for size of a territory, this can vary drastically based on available land and prey, anywhere from 10 to 60 square miles, or even more in the Siberian region. Females are primarily concerned with having a safe place in which to give birth to and rear their cubs, not necessarily securing a large area since it would provide no inherent advantage. Males tend to seek larger areas, which may have to do with greater access to females for mating purposes, as one male might mate with several different females. Additionally, males require a greater input of food, so a larger supply of prey is necessary.

Although tigers are largely solitary, sometimes female tigers will remain with their mother for extended periods or establish territories nearby. Male tigers can become good hunters by the time they are 18 months old, as mentioned earlier, and often leave their mother by two years of age to establish their own territories.

Tigers will chase off transient tigers and other predators from their territories to protect their own hunting grounds from competition. Tigers know their territories well and would prefer not to have others scaring off prey or otherwise causing a distraction. This possessiveness over territory may also be related to mating advantages. If prey is sparse and tigers have to spread out farther, it could decrease the instances of mating and therefore cause a decline in the procreation of the species.

Despite being seen as territorial, tigers don't normally fight one another over territory, unless a wandering tiger in search of its own territory tries to take over another tiger's turf. Besides, why waste time and energy fighting one another when that time and energy would be better spent on hunting prey for the next meal? Fighting between tigers is more often caused by resources, which mainly translates to access to females for mating purposes.

## Counting Tigers

It's estimated that in the early 20th century, there were around 100,000 tigers in the world. There may have been approximately 40,000 tigers in India alone during this time, according to conservationist Valmik Thapar. The lands they occupied were more contiguous than what we see today with patches here and there. Unfortunately during this period in history there was a greater focus on hunting tigers for sport rather than learning about this mysterious creature.

At the same time, scientists back then didn't have the high-tech tools we have today such as radio-collars for tracking tigers' movements and camera traps to catch candid moments. The lack of scientific evidence from the past also makes it difficult to gauge the differences in tiger behavior over time.

Tigers in captivity are not useful specifically for conservation purposes because they are not suited for life in the wild. Many untrained individuals in the US have tigers as pets. There are an estimated 5,000 tigers in the US that are kept as pets, which oddly enough exceeds the number of tigers believed to be in the wild at the time of this writing.

To estimate the number of tigers in a habitat, a variety of techniques can be used. Note that I said *estimate*, as getting an accurate count of tigers in the wild would be nearly impossible, at least not without significant expenditure of time and money. At any rate, one technique that has been used in India is to make traces of paw prints and then try to differentiate between different tigers and come up with a tally. Obviously this is not the most scientific method, so such numbers should be taken with a grain of salt.

Camera traps have also been used, but these are expensive and it's not feasible to put up cameras in every possible location where a tiger might roam. The good thing is that each tiger has a unique set of stripes, so with enough analysis, the number of unique tigers in an area can be tallied, and this sample size can be used to estimate the population over a larger area.

Another strategy is counting prey and estimating the number of tigers that might be in the vicinity, but this might even be less accurate than tracing paw prints. A newer technique is to collect tiger feces and run DNA tests on them to identify unique tigers.

*Let's Talk Numbers*

The World Wildlife Fund (WWF) reported in April of 2016 that 3,890 tigers (or possibly more) are still alive in the wild. This is actually higher than it was at one point, but still an extremely drastic drop from what the figures were in the early 1900s.

There are 13 countries where tigers are believed to still exist in the wild. These tiger range countries are (in alphabetical order): Bangladesh, Bhutan, Cambodia, China, India, Indonesia, Laos, Malaysia, Myanmar (Burma), Nepal, Russia, Thailand, and Vietnam.

The greatest population of tigers is in India. Despite poaching in India, wildlife in general seems to have flourished in this country thanks to conservation efforts and a widespread reverence for nature due to culture and religion.

Following is a breakdown by country of how many tigers exist in the wild according to the WWF data.

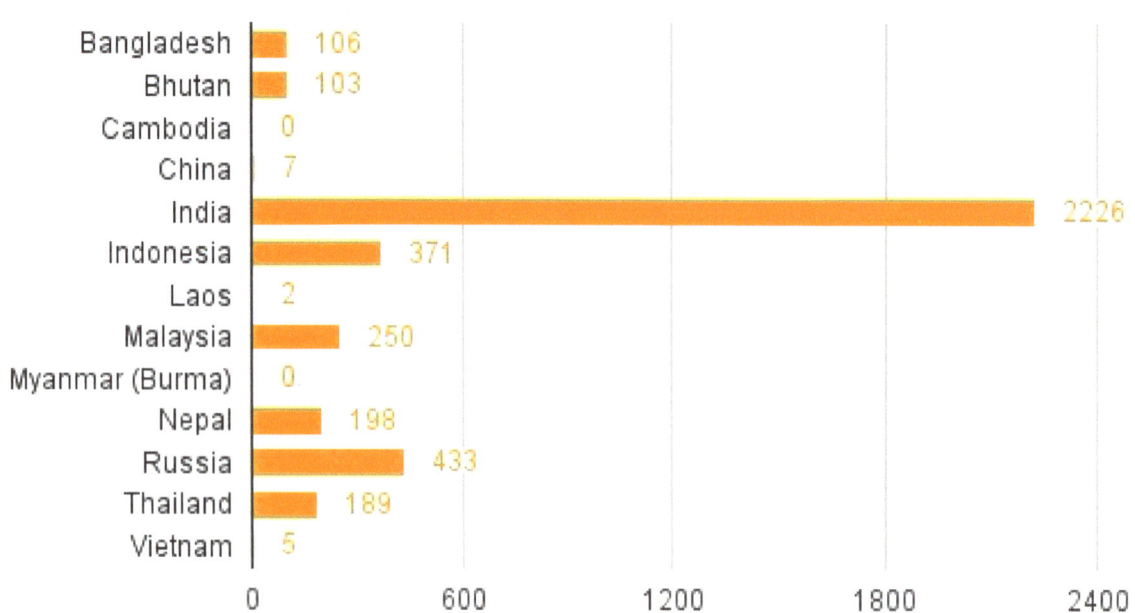

Next is a heat map giving a visual indication of where tigers are highest or lowest in number (with red representing the highest density). Despite China's land mass, the disparity between its tiger numbers and India's couldn't be greater.

Lastly, here's another breakdown by country, but this time showing the tiger population as a percentage of all remaining wild tigers for the six top countries.

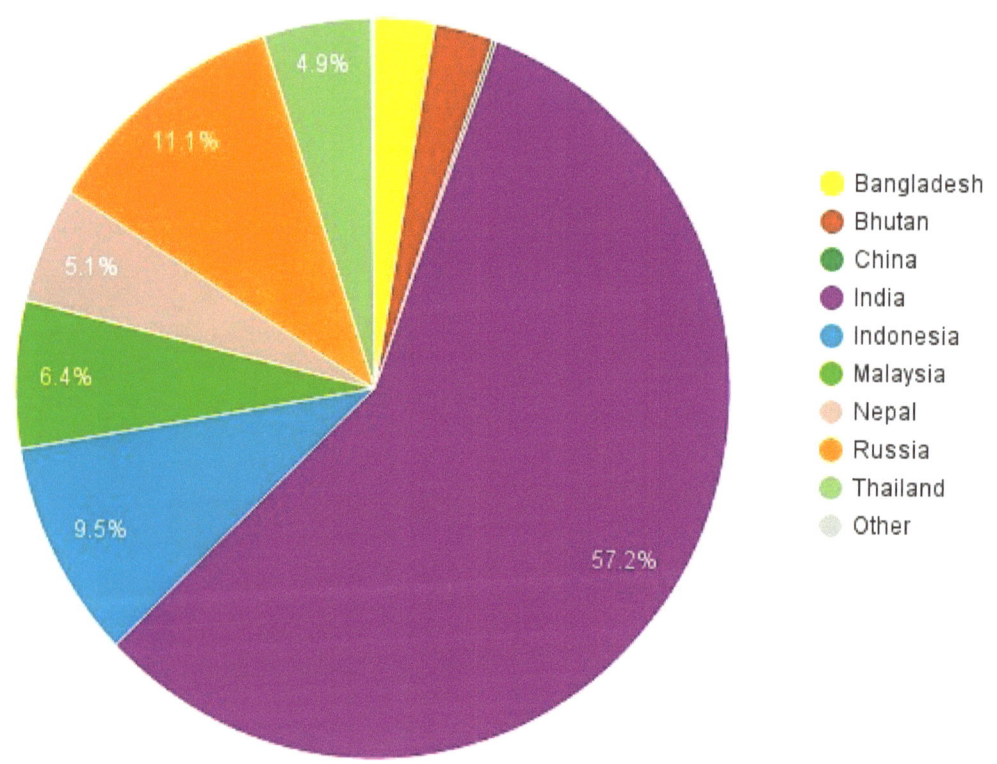

*Threats to its Existence*

There are various reasons for the tiger's decline. One somewhat recent concern is the canine distemper virus that can affect a variety of animals. National Geographic reported in June of 2013 that this disease had affected a number of tigers, even though this is a disease more widely known for affecting dogs, as is indicative by the name. If infected, tigers can suffer from respiratory issues, loss of motor skills, and brain damage.

Speaking of ailments, in traditional Chinese medicine, tiger bones may be ground up and used as an analgesic to relieve pain. In some Asian cultures, it's believed that tiger parts have healing properties. For example, tiger fat for curing leprosy, tiger tail for skin disease, tiger whiskers for toothache, and tiger eyes for -- what else? -- cataracts. The fact that a market exists for tiger parts means some have resorted to dubious methods to obtain and sell such parts.

In addition, the human population is growing and has encroached on the tiger's habitat. This is something we'll have to deal with equitably, as the earth is vast and we need to share it. Governments of tiger range countries will need to step in and create boundaries. It's going to be challenging, though. Unfortunately, some farmers, out of fear for their livestock, have killed tigers. Another issue is the continued development of infrastructure that is fragmenting tiger habitats, such as the building of roads and gas pipelines in Asia.

Furthermore, hunters have killed tigers as prizes out of machismo, especially during colonial periods in Asia when members of royalty would go on hunting escapades. Apparently they considered it brave and courageous to shoot something from a distance (although I wonder how they would have fared going face-to-face with a tiger). Hunters have also over-hunted prey animals that tigers feed on, including deer and wild cattle, meaning less food for tigers' sustenance. Keep in mind that a tiger needs about one deer-sized animal per week in order to survive.

Two of the biggest threats tigers face today are poaching and deforestation. Poachers have

made good money by trapping and hunting the big cat and selling its various parts. Some people want the tiger's fur as some sort of a trophy, and as previously mentioned, in some cultures people believe that consuming tiger parts can have medicinal effects. Trade of these items is illegal, but when so much potential for money is involved, people find a way. It's not much different than drug smuggling. Some folks see the tiger as a commodity and sell it piece by piece. To them, a tiger is more valuable dead than alive.

It's not just the poaching of tigers that's an issue, but the poaching of animals that tigers would use as prey. They are biologically engineered to survive on meat, and a lack of food could mean death by starvation for tigers. There has been a reduction of deer and wild cattle in tiger range countries. Besides poaching, some prey animals have reduced in number for other reasons. For example, wild boar were poisoned in Kazakhstan when rice paddy fields were developed. Not only did this mean less prey for tigers, but perhaps tigers got sick from consuming poisoned boar.

As for deforestation, companies like Asia Pulp & Paper and Unilever have chopped down trees at a rapid rate for paper-making and palm oil. Both companies have made pledges to reduce or eliminate deforestation, but we will have to wait and see if they stay true to their words or if a desire for profits trumps all else. Now that we live in a global economy, food products from these forests are also being scooped up at a faster pace for exporting, such as coffee, tea, herbs, and spices.

In general, there has been too much interference in tiger habitats by hunters, wood-gatherers, etc. It's important that male tigers disperse far and wide to mate with distant females in order to increase the population of tigers. But with a reduction in habitat, some tigers have to attempt crossing inhabited areas or farmland, which puts them at risk of being shot or even poisoned.

Based on all of the above facts, it seems that the tiger has been persecuted in a sense, and that the odds have been stacked against it. If any species was wiped out in massive numbers at a rapid pace, such as what has happened to the tiger, it wouldn't be possible to reproduce fast enough to get the population back to what it was.

## Efforts to Help

India passed a law in 1970 specifically to protect tigers from hunting and from the sale of their skins. Prime Minister Indira Gandhi, who was a staunch conservationist herself, introduced this legislation. However, by 1970, many thousands of tigers had already fallen victim to hunting. India also launched the Wildlife Protection Act in 1972, which aims to protect animal and plant species in general. It prohibits the hunting and killing of all wild animals.

Project Tiger launched in India in 1973, which was supposed to assign one scientist to each reserve within the project. Unfortunately that did not happen, apparently due to political reasons. The goal of Project Tiger was to preserve habitats and maintain a reasonable number of Bengal tigers in the wild. As of January 2017, there are 50 tiger reserves in India.

The main objective for tiger reserves is to provide an environment in which tigers can mate, give birth to cubs, and safely raise them. This requires not only a healthy population of adult male & female tigers, but also adequate food, water, and secluded areas where cubs can be reared (i.e. tiger dens). What's more, conditions must be suitable for prey animals such as deer to flourish.

Another initiative in India created gas connections to nearly 10,000 homes. This resulted in less of a reason for people to seek wood for fuel from the forest and greater preservation of the natural habitat.

Outside of India, there's an international treaty that aims to control the trade of animal parts and plants known as the Convention on International Trade in Endangered Species (CITES). It basically regulates trade, rather than try to prohibit it, and works based on cooperation between governments. It may be impossible to eliminate trade, but being able to track it at least provides some visibility and statistics.

Similar to CITES is a non-governmental organization (NGO) called TRAFFIC, established in 1976, that monitors wildlife and plant trade. In case you're wondering, the acronym stands for Trade Records Analysis of Flora and Fauna in Commerce. Its goal is to control trade in such a manner that it does not negatively impact ecosystems and that a healthy population of wildlife is maintained, while also meeting people's needs for resources and supporting the economy.

These laws and treaties are a step in the right direction, but a big issue is enforcement. Some tiger range areas are patrolled by forest rangers armed with nothing more than sticks. If they are confronted by a gang of poachers armed with guns, they may have no choice but to turn a blind eye out of fear. Plus, it's not feasible to patrol every square inch of these forests.

Thankfully, groups like the Wildlife Conservation Society and World Wildlife Fund have provided resources and manpower to help tiger range countries prevent poaching and have even helped to convict poachers. Conservationists have also gone into rural areas to educate people and discourage the hunting of tigers.

WWF reported in April of 2016 that for the first time in a century, tiger populations finally saw an increase in numbers. It was estimated that there were about 3,200 tigers in the wild in 2010, and nearly 3,900 tigers at the time of this report. India alone saw a 30% increase. This is astounding news that provides hope for the future.

There is an initiative called Tx2, launched in 2010, that aims to double the tiger population by the year 2022. This year was chosen because it is the Year of the Tiger in  Chinese culture. If this goal is successful, there would be about 6,400 tigers in the wild by 2022. Tx2 is an effort that actively involves the governments of all 13 tiger range countries.

## Faith-Based Perspective

As a man of faith, I believe that we are tenants of God's earth, and that we must respect and take care of this world and all its inhabitants. We are only here temporarily, but the earth will continue to spin after our passing. Thus, we must leave this world in the same or better condition than which we found it, such that future generations can exist and have no less a quality of life than what we experienced.

We weren't put here to destroy the earth, or to let our greed or other whims take over to the point of plundering every last drop of benefit that nature provides us with. We are welcome to take advantage of what God has blessed us with on this vast planet, but everything should be done in moderation, whether it's chopping down trees, fishing, or extracting other natural resources.

The Prophet Muhammad (peace be upon him) was quoted as saying: "All creatures are God's family; and God loves most those who treat His family well and kindly." Thus, we should not only treat one another with kindness and respect, but all living things. We should especially speak up for those living things that cannot speak up for themselves. As humans, we've been given the most power and intelligence of all living creatures, but we should see this as more of a responsibility than a privilege.

*Why Bother?*

One may reasonably ask why we should go through so much trouble to conserve the tiger. Even if all tigers in the wild did perish, we would still have many tigers in captivity, whether in zoos or those being kept as pets.

Well, one reason is if you just happen to like this animal. Perhaps you are enamored by its combination of beauty and power, form and function. Another reason is for economic purposes, as tigers do help bring in tourist dollars for countries like India and Thailand. This helps create jobs, empowering people in other parts of the world to make an honest living in the hospitality or travel industries.

One obvious benefit of tourism to tiger range countries is the economic boost those countries receive. Another less obvious benefit is that when tourists go on tiger-seeing tours, it places more eyes and ears on the forest by people who are presumably tiger fans. This could potentially make it more difficult for poachers to carry out their devious deeds. The presence of tourists might also motivate park rangers to do their utmost in protecting and preserving the forests they are responsible for. Tourism is indeed a good thing overall, but care should be taken to not disturb the habitat or wildlife.

There's a bigger reason than admiration for the animal or tourism dollars. It's about more than just saving one animal species. Saving tigers means saving forests and rivers by conserving nature rather than letting it be destroyed. This in turn provides habitat for many other animal and plant species. The fruits and other produce from these forests provide sustenance for locals and for other animals.

Preserving forests means that more trees are available to soak up carbon emissions and other pollutants produced by factories and such. Trees store the carbon, while releasing fresh oxygen for us to breathe. Healthy forests can potentially help fight against climate change. Trees also provide shade and a resting place for birds.

Here's some additional food for thought (no pun intended): After a tiger makes a kill, it consumes a high proportion of the animal within days, leaving bits and pieces that end up being consumed by scavengers (such as wild dogs and vultures) as well as insects and bacterial microbes. Essentially, nothing goes to waste. Even the remains of skin and bone are sucked up by the soil and provide nutrients to plant life, which subsequently act as food for herbivorous animals (i.e. plant eaters). It's the circle of life, as we learned in Disney's *The Lion King*.

All that is involved with saving the tiger ultimately protects the ecosystem, and helps preserve the balance in nature. When cooking, one ingredient can't be eliminated and the same results expected. Likewise, in nature, an important piece of the puzzle can't be eliminated without some sort of downstream impact. Everything in nature works in harmony, and an equilibrium must be maintained.

You see, it's not just about saving the tiger. It's about saving the world.

## Is There Hope?

All hope is not yet lost. Keep in mind that the tiger has survived many centuries. Scientists believe that tigers have roamed the earth for over a million years. Based on fossils that have been discovered, a subspecies known as the Trinil tiger may have inhabited parts of Indonesia as long as 1.2 million years ago.

Even if this figure is off, it goes to show the longevity and persistence of the tiger. Man has hunted and poached the tiger, not to mention destroyed much of its habitat, but a tiger does not go down without a fight. And if we can help through conservation efforts, hopefully the tiger will continue to grace the earth with its presence for many years to come.

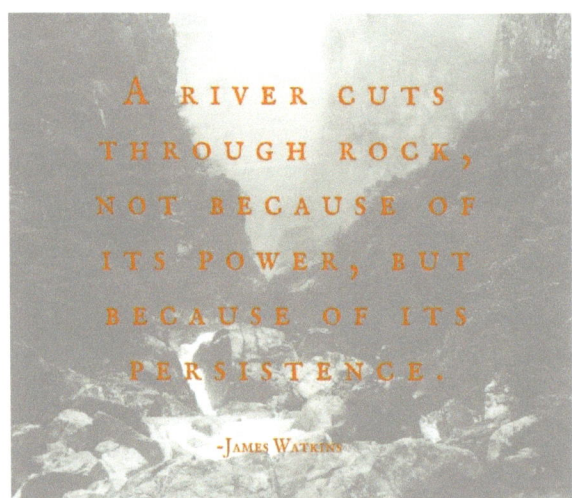

A RIVER CUTS THROUGH ROCK, NOT BECAUSE OF ITS POWER, BUT BECAUSE OF ITS PERSISTENCE.

-JAMES WATKINS

## Conservation Organizations

Big Cat Rescue (bigcatrescue.org)

Panthera (panthera.org)

Wildlife Conservation Society (wcs.org)

World Wildlife Fund (worldwildlife.org)

## References

Karanth, K.U. (2003). *The Way of the Tiger: Natural History and Conservation of the Endangered Big Cat*. Stillwater, MN: Voyageur Press.

Mills, S. (2004). *Tiger*. Buffalo, NY: Firefly Books.

Park, S. (2015). *Great Soul of Siberia: Passion, Obsession, and One Man's Quest for the World's Most Elusive Tiger*. Vancouver, BC: Greystone Books.

Sunquist, F., & Sunquist, M. (2014). *The Wild Cat Book*. Chicago, IL: The University of Chicago Press.

*Charts/graphs created by author in Google Sheets.*

*All tiger photos obtained from pexels.com with Creative Commons Zero (CC0) license.*

www.ingramcontent.com/pod-product-compliance
Lightning Source LLC
Chambersburg PA
CBHW041521280526

45792CB00004B/1328